# 2017
# SPEAKER SHOWCASE

## WORKBOOK:
## KANSAS CITY

Presented by Nancy & Bill Lauterbach

2017 Speaker Showcase: Kansas City

*Red*Propeller, LLC
*A Bill & Nancy Lauterbach Company*

*Red**Propeller*, LLC

**A Bill & Nancy Lauterbach Company**

RedPropeller, LLC
10087 E. Ironwood Dr. Scottsdale, AZ 85258
(480) 366-4040
http://www.redpropellerusa.com
email: nancy@redprops.com



Manufactured in the United States of America

2017 Speaker Showcase: Kansas City

Future Showcases: www.RedPropShowcase.com

Supreme Commander:  Nancy Lauterbach
Showcase Executive Producer: Jeff Slutsky (jeff@StreetFighterMarketing.com)
Cover & Interior Production & Design: Susan McDonald (susan@intuitivecreator.com)

ISBN-13: 978-1978439283
ISBN-10: 1978439288

# Contents

# The Many Benefits of a Speaker Showcase

## By Nancy Lauterbach

*Finding the perfect speaker on the perfect topic for the perfect fee can be an imperfect process. Spending countless hours reviewing video after video is time consuming and still may not be the most "accurate" representation of how a certain speaker performs in front of the audience. The solution? Attending a speaker showcase.*

The speaker showcase is a special event where as many as 23 speakers present 15-20 minutes of their material in front on an audience of meeting professionals and people who hire speakers. The showcases offered by speaker bureaus is often the most useful because the bureau is not "pushing" any particular speaker. But rather, they are showcasing a number of different speakers on topics and in fee ranges that most meeting professionals most want to review.

**Saves You Time.**

A big key advantage of the showcase is that you get to see all these different speakers at one time. It might take you 23 different trips to see these same speakers live in front of an audience if they happen to be presenting at a location that's reasonably close to you. But the showcase shows them one right after another. Also, seeing these speakers all in the same day gives you a much better way to compare styles and approaches so you can better determine which speakers make the most sense for your objectives and goals for those meetings and conventions that need professional outside talent to maximize the results of your efforts.

**Gives You a More Accurate Picture.**

The standard tool for choosing speakers is the video. But a video may not be the most "honest" representation. With clever editing and advanced post production techniques, it's possible that the video may give the impression that a speaker is better (or perhaps different) than he or she actually is in front of an audience. At the showcase you see for yourself just how that speaker performs.

  PH: 913-488-6480    EMAIL: NANCY@REDPROPS.COM

### You See Their Best.

With only 15-20 minutes, the speaker needs to present those segments of his or her presentation that demonstrates the content, style and stage presence. No need to sit through an entire presentation or view a one-hour video. You'll know in the first 5-10 minutes if this speaker is a potential fit for your events. There is no substitute for seeing a speaker in person.

### Hob Nob with the Speakers.

At a showcase you also get to network directly with the speakers. This is your opportunity to see if the person on the platform is the same person off the platform. This is good to know so when your audience members interact with your speaker before and after the presentation, you feel confident that you hired a professional who is willing to share and provide benefit throughout their visit, not just the time on the platform. You'll also have an opportunity to ask questions and make sure that this speaker can deliver the message you want and how the speaker may be to work with.

### You'll Have Fun and Win Prizes.

In just one day you'll be able to see a group of speakers that collectively charge hundreds of thousands of dollars. The energy in the room is palpable and most showcases offer door prizes throughout which often includes items like books and videos donated by the speakers. Plus, it's a day away from the office doing important research for your next events.

### The Speaker Bureau Advantage.

By attending a showcase presented by Red Propeller Speakers and Trainers you will have an additional resource. You may see a speaker on the showcase you loved but his or her fee may be too much for your budget. Our bureau account executives would then be in a position to perhaps find other speakers they know who were not on the showcase but offer a similar type of presentation more in line with your budget. Or, sometimes there are special circumstances when a speaker may be able to be a little more flexible with the fee and Red Propeller Speakers Bureau is in a position to see if there is a way to make it work for you. Our bureau agents can also help negotiate additional value for you like having the speakers provide articles for your newsletter or blogs in advance of your event. A huge value for working with a good bureau like Red Propeller Speakers and Trainers is that your agent can also negotiate break out sessions for a small additional fee. Since the speaker is already on sight and there is no additional travel, you might be able to offer your attendees a very high caliber workshop for the same cost as an industry speaker.

# The Schedule

Registration
Opening Remarks

Lunch
Prize Drawings

**Group 1**

Speaker 1
Speaker 2
Speaker 3
Speaker 4
Speaker 5

Break
Prize Drawings

**Group 4**

Speaker 14
Speaker 15
Speaker 16
Speaker 17

Break
Prize Drawings

**Group 5**

Speaker 18
Speaker 19
Speaker 20
Speaker 21

Break 4
5th Prize Drawings

**Group 2**

Speaker 6
Speaker 7
Speaker 8
Speaker 9

Break
Prize Drawings

**Group 3**

Speaker 10
Speaker 11
Speaker 12
Speaker 13

**Group 6**

Speaker 22
Speaker 23
Speaker 24
Speaker 25

# THE RED**PROPELLER** TEAM

**NANCY LAUTERBACH**
**PARTNER &**
**SR. ACCOUNT EXECUTIVE**

Email:
Nancy@redprops.com
Ph: 913.488.6480

**NANCY L. RODGERS**
**COMPTROLLER**

Email:
Nancyr@redprops.com

**BILL LAUTERBACH,**
**PARTNER**

Email:
Bill@redprops.com
Ph: 913.706.0241

**BETH HAWLEY**
**DIRECTOR OF**
**COMMUNICATIONS**

Email:
Beth@redprops.com
Ph: 913.244.2510

**SUSAN LAUTERBACH**
**ACCOUNT EXECUTIVE**

Email:
Susan@redprops.com
Ph: (630) 390-6981

**HELENE EICHENWALD**
**LOGISTICS**

*"The Queen of Everything"*
Email:
Helene@redprops.com
Ph: 913.579.5557

**JAMES BAUCHAM**
**ACCOUNT EXECUTIVE**

Email:
James@redprops.com
Ph: (816) 763-5595

**GINA DAVILLA**
**ACCOUNT EXECUTIVE,**
**EXCLUSIVE REP FOR BILLY**
**RIGGS AND JEFF SLUTSKY**

Email:
Gina@redprops.com
Ph: 956.251.3622

# Name That Speaker!

## FILL IN MISSING LETTERS TO FIND THE PERFECT SPEAKER

 PH: 913-488-6480    EMAIL: NANCY@REDPROPS.COM

# Is finding the right speaker puzzling?

```
S  S  S  O  B  L  M  E  O  C  R  E  D  A
I  X  D  U  R  U  L  P  N  O  E  U  N  R
N  A  T  N  S  E  O  I  R  I  F  B  O  O
N  Z  N  H  E  C  C  I  R  S  F  A  M  N
E  B  T  T  S  H  P  N  G  C  E  N  D  I
D  A  I  I  H  A  O  G  A  D  I  K  E  N
Q  D  P  R  H  O  I  C  A  P  H  S  R  M
T  E  X  S  O  R  N  E  H  A  C  A  V  A
M  C  K  I  N  L  E  Y  W  C  S  L  A  R
H  C  A  B  R  E  T  U  A  L  I  O  U  T
D  N  A  L  Y  E  N  M  A  C  K  E  Y  I
K  A  M  P  S  L  U  T  S  K  Y  Y  K  N
H  S  N  I  A  T  W  A  L  L  A  H  B  Z
G  X  N  H  A  C  F  N  S  T  A  L  P  C
```

| | | |
|---|---|---|
| ANTHONY | EUBANKS | REDMOND |
| ARONIN | FINE | RIGGS |
| BHALLA | KAMP | SALO |
| BIRO | LAUTERBACH | SCHIEFFER |
| BUTZ | MACKEY | SHAPIRO |
| CAHN | MARTIN | ~~SLUTSKY~~ |
| COHEN | MCKINLEY | STALP |
| CRILL | MUSHTAQ | TAINSH |
| EPISCOPO | PANCERO | |

*SOLUTION ON PAGE 64*

# MICHAEL C. ANTHONY
## *Body Language Expert*

### SHUT UP & Sell With Your Body

Michael C. Anthony is a best selling author and body language guru. He is a frequent TV guest and discusses the non-verbal communication of business, sales, and politics. His hilarious and interactive keynote, Shut Up & Sell With Your Body will give you an unfair advantage in market place. 55% of all communication is non-verbal, 38% is our tone of voice and only 7% is the actual words we use.

When you master the art of Body Language you will improve your own communication skills and know what the other person is REALLY thinking.

In this keynote you will discover:
- What body language will show others you are an expert
- The different types of handshakes and what they mean
- How to determine what the eyes are really saying
- How to motivate and persuade others to your way of thinking
- How to detect a liar
- The most important body language tactic you could ever use

And much, much more!

### *Michael's Most Popular Topics:*
- Shut Up & Sell With Your Body
- The Totally Mental Makeover

*"Michael, I have to let you know how much we enjoyed having you speak at our annual conference. Both of your presentations inspired us and blew us away at the same time. You were the perfect choice."*

**- Walmart**

  PH: 913-488-6480    EMAIL: NANCY@REDPROPS.COM

**MY NOTES ON MICHAEL C. ANTHONY:** ______________________________

______________________________________________________________

______________________________________________________________

______________________________________________________________

______________________________________________________________

______________________________________________________________

______________________________________________________________

______________________________________________________________

______________________________________________________________

______________________________________________________________

______________________________________________________________

______________________________________________________________

______________________________________________________________

______________________________________________________________

______________________________________________________________

______________________________________________________________

______________________________________________________________

**OUR EVENTS THAT MIGHT BE A GOOD FIT FOR MICHAEL:** _______________

______________________________________________________________

______________________________________________________________

______________________________________________________________

______________________________________________________________

TRAVELS FROM:
Tampa, FL

# MICHAEL ARONIN

## *He makes Disability Funny*

Michael Aronin is a nationally acclaimed speaker who teaches his audiences how to get past personal shortcomings and move forward productively in their careers. Being both a comedian and motivational speaker, he is able to make this difficult topic both entertaining and enlightening.

Michael knows two things: he's got a killer sense of humor, and he's got cerebral palsy. But Michael never let his disability get him down - in fact it hardly even fazed him. While an undergraduate at Towson State University, he was elected President of the Student Government Association. He went on to be one of the hardest working comics in the country.

His outstanding efforts have been recognized by such prominent media sources as ABC TV, CBS TV, NBC TV, Fox Television, The Baltimore Sun, and The Baltimore Business Journal. Michael will captivate your audience and provide them with a new positive outlook on setting and obtaining goals.

As a physically challenged member of the business community, Michael provides a new perspective for overcoming obstacles that goes far beyond "textbook knowledge." Combining his personal experience with existing facts, Michael makes an impact on his audiences in a way that lifts their spirits and motivates them to improve their abilities in the workplace without apprehension, while making them smile.

## *Michael's Most Popular Topic:*

- Walking the Talk, Well Kind Of.

*"Michael Aronin is a dear friend and an incredibly talented speaker. In case you weren't able to hear his presentation yesterday afternoon, he has a unique ability to relate to people, eliminate barriers, and inspire all of us to be our very best."*

**- Jeff Concepcion**
**CEO Stratos Wealth Partners**

**My Notes On Michael Aronin:** ___________________________

_____________________________________________________

_____________________________________________________

_____________________________________________________

_____________________________________________________

_____________________________________________________

_____________________________________________________

_____________________________________________________

_____________________________________________________

_____________________________________________________

_____________________________________________________

_____________________________________________________

_____________________________________________________

_____________________________________________________

_____________________________________________________

_____________________________________________________

**Our events that might be a good fit for Michael:** ___________________

_____________________________________________________

_____________________________________________________

_____________________________________________________

_____________________________________________________

_____________________________________________________

_____________________________________________________

TRAVELS FROM:
Baltimore, MD

# Gaurav Bhalla, Ph.D.

*Visionary Leadership Trainer-Speaker-Coach*

### *Soulful Leadership™*

Globally acclaimed training specialist, coach, and author Gaurav Bhalla offers a new visionary leadership training system, Soulful Leadership™. Powered by 40+ years of experience working with the world's top leaders and organizations, like Citi, Deloitte, Microsoft, and JLL, the Soulful Leadership™ training and coaching system helps next generations leaders achieve their transformative potential, and inspires them to lead with their wiser selves – their humanity. Relevant for current and future leaders in all organizations of civic society – corporations, non-profit, associations, education, healthcare, government – it's the difference between leadership being a liability, or an asset for promoting growth, wellbeing and prosperity of all major stakeholders.

Gaurav Bhalla, Ph.D., is a world-class 'thinker-doer, present-ainer' who delivers insight-packed experiences that inspire, entertain, and motivate next-day executive action. He has changed the lives of thousands of executives by inspiring them to hear and see differently the worlds in which they live and operate.

## *Gaurav's Most Popular Topics:*

- Reigniting Trust with Soulful Leadership™
- How Diversity and Collaboration Build Smarter Organizations
- Jumpstart Innovation by Invigorating Your Innovation Culture

*"Gaurav is one of the most engaging speakers I've seen … and I've seen quite a few. The way in which he balances wisdom, insight, poetry, and humor is a rare gift that will leave you wanting more. It is without an ounce of hesitation that I recommend Gaurav Bhalla for your next presentation, facilitation, training, or keynote address. This man delivers."*

**- Steve Dorfman, CEO, Driven to Excel**

**My Notes On Gaurav Bhalla:** _______________________________

**Our events that might be a good fit for Gaurav:** _______________

TRAVELS FROM:
Washington, DC

# Brian Biro

Brian Biro is **America's Breakthrough Coach!** He has delivered over 1,600 presentations around the world over the last 25 years. A major client described Brian best when he said, "Brian Biro has the **energy of a ten-year-old**, the **enthusiasm of a twenty-year-old**, and the **wisdom of a seventy-five-year-old.**" A former vice-president of a major transportation corporation and the author of 11 books including bestseller, Beyond Success!

Brian was **rated #1 from over 40 Speakers** at 4 consecutive INC. Magazine International Conferences. In his first career, Brian built one of the most successful competitive swimming programs in the country and received the United States Swimming Coaching Excellence award. Forty-four of his swimmers earned full college scholarships. With degrees from Stanford University and UCLA, Brian has appeared on Good Morning America, CNN, FOX and as a featured speaker at the Disney Institute in Orlando. **Brian was recently named one of the top 100 most inspirational graduates in the history of the UCLA Graduate School of Business. He was also honored as one of the top 65 Motivational Speakers in the world!**

## *Brian's Most Popular Topics:*

- Breakthrough Leadership!
- Champions of CHANGE!
- From Silos to Synergy!

*"Our GMs did not talk about anything but you and their experience with you, at the party last night. I have been with TGI Fridays for 19 years and I have never seen such a reaction and connection from our people. Thank you for giving of yourself so unselfishly - you have a profound impact!"*

**- Betsy Murphy, VP TGI Fridays**

**PH: 913-488-6480     EMAIL: NANCY@REDPROPS.COM**

**MY NOTES ON BRIAN BIRO:** ______________________________

_______________________________________________________

_______________________________________________________

_______________________________________________________

_______________________________________________________

_______________________________________________________

_______________________________________________________

_______________________________________________________

_______________________________________________________

_______________________________________________________

_______________________________________________________

_______________________________________________________

_______________________________________________________

_______________________________________________________

_______________________________________________________

_______________________________________________________

_______________________________________________________

**OUR EVENTS THAT MIGHT BE A GOOD FIT FOR BRIAN:** ______________________

_______________________________________________________

_______________________________________________________

_______________________________________________________

_______________________________________________________

_______________________________________________________

_______________________________________________________

_______________________________________________________

TRAVELS FROM:
Asheville, NC

# TRACY BUTZ

## *North America's Premier Speaker on Workplace Culture*

As a former Director of Learning & Development, TRACY BUTZ was accountable for talent management and employee development. She parlayed her career to become one of the most sought after speakers on the topic of workplace culture. Tracy knows how to design a workplace culture employees love and empower high performance. She delivers interactive, fun and results-focused workshops.

Tracy holds the designation of Certified Speaking Professional™ (CSP), which is the highest honor in the speaking profession, held by only 12% of speakers worldwide. In addition to her brilliant speaking career, she is a prolific and accomplished author that is supported by her bestselling book *HOLY COW!* Her clients are a who's who list of organizations both large and small. Tracy Butz is a speaker who understands client needs, delivers on her promises, and is your solution to energize your workplace.

### *Tracy's Most Popular Topics:*

- HOLY COW!® Create an Amazing Workplace that Steers Passion, Performance & Prosperity
- Be the Architect for Your Life! Dream It. Plan It. Live It.
- Tame the Turbulence: Avoid Losing It. Fly Through It.

*Tracy has a natural grace and comfort that allowed her points to connect and resonate with our audience of 500+ attendees. Numerous survey sheets had her comments as the one thing they would take home from the convention and put into practice. This tells me her presentation was well received and life changing. She did exactly what we expected , which was to enhance the lives of those who attended. Thank you to Tracy, as the audience loved her.*

**- Jeff Harrold, Chairman & CEO,
Auto-Owners Insurance**

**My Notes On Tracy Butz:** _______________________________

**Our events that might be a good fit for Tracy:** _______________

**TRAVELS FROM:**
Denver CO

# Lu Ann Cahn

## *"Dare to Do the New!"*

Every single day for a year, Lu Ann Cahn did something new she'd never done before to get her life unstuck. She zip lined across a crocodile infested lake, spent a day in a wheelchair and ate a scorpion. She did things she never imagined she would do and her life opened up in amazing ways.

Today this 8 time Emmy award winning journalist, cancer survivor and author dares audiences across the country to go on their own unique journey; to Do The New and move courageously toward change.

Audiences laugh and sometimes cry as this master story teller engages audiences with an inspiring and interactive presentation.

Lu Ann has been featured on the Today Show, EXTRA, CNN Headline News and BBC Radio. Her book, *I Dare Me*, published by a division of Penguin, has been translated into Chinese and has attracted readers and fans all over the world.

### *Lu Ann's Most Popular Topics:*

- I Dare Me for Leaders, Corporate Meetings, Associations, Conferences
- I Dare Me for Survivors and Caregivers
- I Dare Me for Career Counseling Professionals, Life Coaches, Counselors
- I Dare Me for Fundraising: The Karmic Giveback

*We had a waiting list for people who wanted to get into our sold out luncheon featuring Lu Ann Cahn and her I Dare Me presentation "Living Fearlessly". Her daring and inspiring speech lived up to all reviews and beyond. Our business women and men laughed out loud and related to her story of being stuck and surviving cancer. Lu Ann moves into the crowd and gets everyone participating, shouting out their dares. We pride ourselves on getting the finest speakers in the region. She was definitely one of our best!*

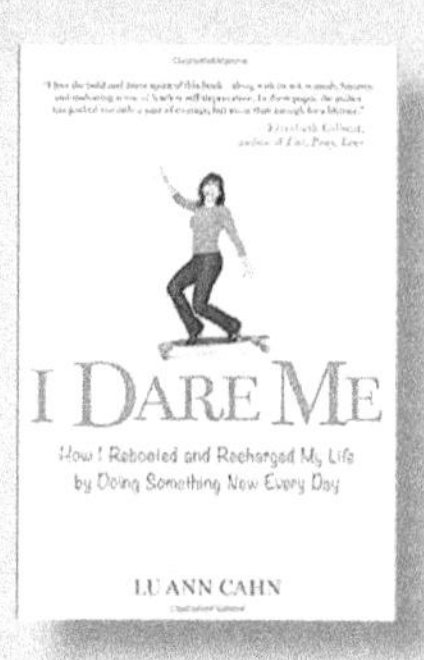

**- Eileen Connolly-Robbins**
**Founder, Society of Professional Women**

**MY NOTES ON LU ANN CAHN:** ________________________________

________________________________________________________________

________________________________________________________________

________________________________________________________________

________________________________________________________________

________________________________________________________________

________________________________________________________________

________________________________________________________________

________________________________________________________________

________________________________________________________________

________________________________________________________________

________________________________________________________________

________________________________________________________________

________________________________________________________________

________________________________________________________________

________________________________________________________________

________________________________________________________________

**OUR EVENTS THAT MIGHT BE A GOOD FIT FOR LU ANN:** ________________

________________________________________________________________

________________________________________________________________

________________________________________________________________

________________________________________________________________

________________________________________________________________

________________________________________________________________

________________________________________________________________

________________________________________________________________

TRAVELS FROM:
Philadelphia, PA

# Aimee Cohen

## *"The Career Dream-Maker*

Aimee Cohen is the "Career Dream-Maker!" With all of the training and education you receive to do your job, you have never had anyone teach you how to create a life-long, fulfilling, and successful career...until now! Time to pull on your "big-girl panties" and take control of your career.

After more than 20 years and a nearly 100% success rate as an elite career coach, Aimee shares all of her secrets, strategies, tips, tools, processes, and practical action steps to catapult your career. From personal branding and navigating office politics to overcoming self-sabotaging behavior and elevating your executive presence, Aimee arms you with the information you need to not only achieve, but exceed your professional goals. Whether it's your first position or a C-suite position, achieving professional success is about having an edge.

Today's workplace is more competitive than ever, and that's why you need Aimee Cohen to empower you to Woman UP!

### *Aimee's Most Popular Topics:*

- Woman UP! Overcome the 7 Deadly Sins that Sabotage Your Success
- Manage Your Career Like a Boss
- Polish Your Executive Presence and Skyrocket Your Career

*"Aimee is empowering and inspiring...her Woman UP! message combines your best girlfriend and an elite career expert in one powerful package!"*

*"Aimee's advice is easy to follow and gets results!"*

**- Teresa Taylor,
former COO Qwest Communications,
and author of *The Balance Myth***

   

**My Notes On Aimee Cohen:**

**Our events that might be a good fit for Aimee:**

TRAVELS FROM:
Denver, CO

# Linda Crill

*Inspiring. Irreverent. Impassioned.*

A former Fortune 100 executive, Linda Crill is recognized as a worldwide authority on change management. She is engaged in speaking, training and facilitating change projects around the world helping thousands of leaders at companies such as Citigroup, Honeywell International and Marriott.

Linda is a masterful author with an ability to influence people through her words and ideas. In her award-winning book *Blind Curves*, she traded her corporate suits for motorcycle leathers and signed up for a 2,500-mile road trip riding a Harley. Her unusual story of reinvention shows the value of erasing old boundaries and opening doors labeled "not me."

Linda's colorful and diverse employment background in government, nonprofit and corporate America has helped her gain a perspective that most business owners have never experienced. She shares these perspectives with her audiences.

Linda's persistence, determination and willingness to change is evidenced by her interests that include downhill skiing, trapeze flying, scuba diving, and ballroom dancing.

She is the mother of 3 grown children who wholeheartedly support her nontraditional zest for life. As a widow, caregiver and cancer survivor, Linda shares a powerful message of resilience and reinvention when asking, "What now?"

## Linda's Most Popular Topics:

- **What Now?** Creating Change to Stay Competitive
- **Innovation:** Unlocking New Value
- **Blind Curves** – How to Be Resilient in Times of Change

*"It's easy to feel overwhelmed in a world that changes faster than any of us can keep up. Linda's stories shake up traditional ways of handling the unexpected, erasing old boundaries and moving ahead of the competition."*

**- Cynthia de Lorenzi, CEO, Success in the City**

**My Notes On Linda Crill:** ___________________________________________

**Our events that might be a good fit for Linda:** _______________________

TRAVELS FROM:
Washington DC

# Matt Episcopo

*Speaker • Author • Coach*

Matt Episcopo, a highly decorated law enforcement veteran, effectively teaches how to connect and make a positive and powerful first impression that will build trust and confidence upon first meeting. Learn how to have an unfair advantage and communicate by using the same techniques as FBI Hostage Negotiators, and convert meetings into relationships for business and life.

During his 21+ year career in law enforcement, Matt Episcopo rose to the rank of Captain by developing ground-breaking programs and due to his excellence in leadership. He received numerous awards and citations during this time including: the Medal of Honor, Meritorious Service, Gallantry Star, Honorable Service, and Outstanding Law Enforcement Officer of the Year. Matt has become an international author, speaker and coach. He continues to mentor new police recruits, while training people to master their leadership and communication skills.

Matt's energy will light up the room and keep your attendees on the edge of their seat, hanging on his every word. The information that Matt shares are easy to learn, can be done by anybody, and is proven to work. Matt's presentations are engaging and interactive so that the attendees experience a high retention rate.

## Matt's Most Popular Topics:

- **How to Gain the Upper Hand,** P.O.W.E.R Tactics that Get Leaders Results
- **How To Create A Point Of Impact:** Build confidence, trust and rapport in under 10 seconds by using this secret sequence used by expert interrogators
- **Secrets of Body Language:** Learn how to see 80% more than you do now and use it to your advantage.

*"Matt was such a hit with attendees last year. He delivered an unbelievable amount of content- real world, workable tools and strategies. His persuasion strategies were through the roof. The great thing about working with Matt is that you don't have to worry. As a producer, I've got a lot of things going on in my mind when I put on an event. With Matt, I never have to worry- he promises and then he delivers, over-delivers and then delivers some more. If you're looking for someone to bring to your event, I would feel comfortable giving a whole hearted 110% recommendation to whatever Matt offers."*

**- Brad Ross, Producer: IT Factor Live**

**My Notes On Matt Espiscopo:** ______________________

_______________________________________________________

_______________________________________________________

_______________________________________________________

_______________________________________________________

_______________________________________________________

_______________________________________________________

_______________________________________________________

_______________________________________________________

_______________________________________________________

_______________________________________________________

_______________________________________________________

_______________________________________________________

_______________________________________________________

_______________________________________________________

_______________________________________________________

_______________________________________________________

**Our events that might be a good fit for Matt:** ______________

_______________________________________________________

_______________________________________________________

_______________________________________________________

_______________________________________________________

_______________________________________________________

TRAVELS FROM:
Syracuse, NY

# Bob Eubanks

### *"One of a Kind"*

I'm sure when you hear the name Bob Eubanks, you think of the Newlywed Game. But, why not? TV guide named him one of the top five game show hosts of all time. He's an eight time Emmy award winner with a star on the Hollywood Walk of Fame. But, boy are you in for a surprise.

There are television producers, concert producers, and artist managers, but only one person in the entire entertainment industry has done it all.

He produced concerts for the Beatles, Rolling Stones, and Merle Haggard. He managed the careers of Dolly Parton and Barbara Mandrell. He produced television shows for all three major networks. And, he also has a unique business philosophy which has made him one of the most successful entrepreneurs in the entertainment industry.

He's one of a kind.

## Bob's Most Popular Topics:

- Relationships at home and in the workplace
- How to take your strengths and apply them to other areas in the workplace
- The importance of maintaining good people skills in a technological world

*"Before the Awards show, a couple of fellow board members questioned the idea of showing clips from The Newlywed Game. They didn't understand the relevance to the public relations industry. After the show they had nothing but praise about how entertaining the clips were, but more importantly, about how you really understood the audience and managed to tie in the clips to our profession so beautifully!"*

**- Rita Tateel, President, The Celebrity Source, Inc.**

**My Notes On Bob Eubanks:** _______________________________________

_______________________________________________________________

_______________________________________________________________

_______________________________________________________________

_______________________________________________________________

_______________________________________________________________

_______________________________________________________________

_______________________________________________________________

_______________________________________________________________

_______________________________________________________________

_______________________________________________________________

_______________________________________________________________

_______________________________________________________________

_______________________________________________________________

_______________________________________________________________

**Our events that might be a good fit for Bob:** _______________________

TRAVELS FROM:
Los Angeles, CA

# DEBRA FINE

### *Internationally Recognized Conversation and Networking Expert*

Bestselling author, keynote speaker and trainer, Fine began her career as an engineer, an occupation that allowed her to maintain her natural shyness and avoid situations that required social and personal interactions. Now a long time member of the National Speakers Association she presents to and trains audiences across the globe. Fine designs her presentations and researches her books to teach audiences conversation skills and business networking techniques that develop business relationships, enhance visibility, gain referrals and build rapport in the workplace. Fine's highly informative, entertaining and interactive programs offer concrete tools for making the most of meetings, networking opportunities and face to face interactions in an online world.

Debra's bestselling books: The Fine Art of Small Talk: How to Start a Conversation, Keep It Going, Build Networking Skills—and Leave a Positive Impression (Hachette), The Fine Art of the Big Talk: How to Win Clients, Deliver Great Presentations, and Solve Conflicts at Work (Hachette) have been translated and published in over 2 dozen countries around the world. Just released is Debra's third in the "Fine Art" series: Beyond Texting: The Fine Art of Face-to-Face Communication for Teenagers (Canon). A regular Huffington Post blogger, Fine's recent media appearances include The Today Show, CNN, The Early Show, CBS Sunday Morning, Fox Business News and NPR Morning Edition.

### *Debra's Most Popular Topics:*

- The Fine Art of Building Business Relationships and Expanding Networks
- The Fine Art of Small Talk: Every Conversation is an Opportunity for Success
- The Fine Art of Leadership: One Conversation at a Time

*"Our group of 500 participants thought you were wonderful. They loved the topic and your wonderfully energetic and amusing delivery. Many people told me we should have given you twice as much time. In the eight years that we have sponsored this conference you have proved to be our most popular luncheon speaker. The response was simply overwhelming"*

**My Notes On Debra Fine:**

**Our events that might be a good fit for Debra:**

TRAVELS FROM:
Denver, CO

# MARVELLESS MARK KAMP
## *Keynote Entertainer/Business Rock Star*

Mark works with organizations that want their teams to achieve rock star results.

Take your business from garage band to in demand with Mark Kamp's fun and easily applied four solid rock success principals that come directly from rock stars. ,Teams will get immediate results when action is taken, and Mark will make you the rock star in the eyes of your peers. Music is multi generational and so is Opportunity Rocks. Mark has been delivering rock star results for his clients since starting his business in 2001. A real renaissance man, Mark combines entertainment, high content and a high level of engagement to create events that become memorable experiences. Mark leaves his audiences feeling like rock stars themselves - Rock stars who are equipped with new strategies, tactics, techniques and ideas that exceed expectations in their workplace. As a keynote speaker he presents, entertains and inspires making him a great speaker for the hard to fill spots.  Mark can also serve as Master of Ceremony's for  ROI to keep the energy high.

Mark is the author of "Opportunity Rocks: Be a Rockstar in Business and Beyond" and has been featured in US Today. TBN, Small Business Trendsetters, Business Innovators and more.

Marvelless Mark Kamp's rock star clientele include: Microsoft, NEW York Life, BMW, Disney, The American Cancer Society, Sony, McDonalds, Oracle, Marriott, American Express and many more.

### *Mark's Most Popular Topics:*

- **Opportunity Rocks:** From Garage Band To In Demand
- **Opportunity Rocks:** Building Your Rock Star Teams, For Rock Star Results
- **Rhythms In Business:** Beating The Competition, Drumming Up Business Depending On Your Band

*"Mark captures the essence of what it takes to stand out like the legendary music rock stars.  After his presentation, my team and I experienced a renewed energy and a new way of thinking about performing at higher levels on a daily basis to achieve overall success in our department."*

**- Mary Ellen Grom, VP of Marketing
Synnex Corporation.**

**My Notes On Mark Kamp:** ____________________

**Our events that might be a good fit for Mark Kamp:** ____________

TRAVELS FROM:
Las Vegas, NV

# JACK MACKEY

"You can market all you want, but people BELIEVE what they experience!" So says Jack Mackey, Chief Evangelist at SMG, the leading customer analytics agency helping organizations drive growth through customer loyalty. His high-energy presentations are packed with actionable customer insights, laugh-out-loud humor, and repeatable success stories from decades of SMG loyalty research.

Jack says, "There are only three ways to grow a going concern:  1) retain the customers you have now, 2) get your current customers to spend more or, 3) get more new customers.  You can accomplish all three, at the same time, by delivering a loyalty-inspiring customer experience.

Loyal customers not only keep doing business with you, they spend more, and send new customers your way through the positive stories they tell about doing business with you.  Plus, loyalty protects you like armor against competition because a great customer experience is the hardest thing for rivals to copy."

## Jack's Most Popular Topics:

- **What Customers Love (and what service leaders must know and do about it)**
- **Activating a Vibrant Net Promoter System (NPS) to Lead the Field**
- **Attract Great Customers, Win Passionate Loyalty & Drive True Growth**

*"Jack Mackey was so instrumental in the success of our conference it is hard to put it into words. He deeply captured the attention of our attendees regarding the power of customer experience. Most importantly, he presented in a way that was so relatable the audience was laughing one minute and crying the next and furiously scribbling notes in between. I would highly recommend Jack for any conference or speaking event."*

**- Susan Hern, Director of Operations, Nothing Bundt Cakes**

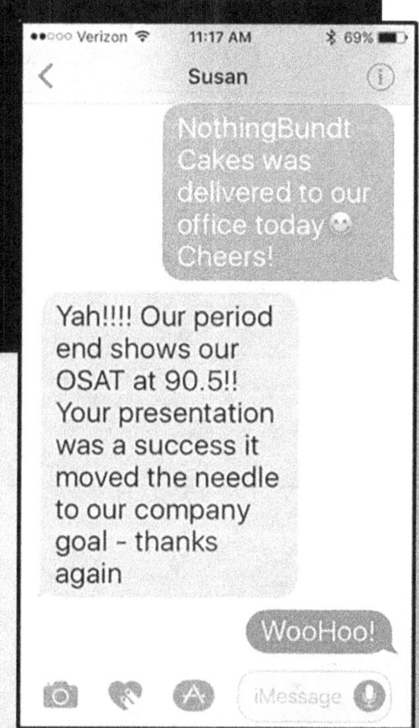

**MY NOTES ON JACK MACKEY:**

**OUR EVENTS THAT MIGHT BE A GOOD FIT FOR JACK:**

TRAVELS FROM:
Kansas City, MO

# DAVE MARTIN
## *Your Success Coach*

Dave Martin, Your Success Coach, inspires and equips individuals and corporations to pursue success in personal life and in business. Using principle based coaching and transformative thinking, Dave has been a mentor, a leader, and an inspirational and motivational speaker for over 25 years. He shares timeless truths, wrapped in humor and delivered with passion, coaching people to possess a life of success and to create the groundwork for an enduring legacy.

Dave engages his audience with interactive methods of learning and is focused on changing ingrained thought patterns and expanding the conventional mindset. Based in Orlando, Florida, Dave is booked domestically and internationally for corporate speaking events, seminars and keynotes. He is also the author of several best-selling books including The 12 Traits of the Greats, and Another Shot. Thousands have invested in his personal coaching systems and participate in Dave's free weekly podcast, Success Made Simple.

Dave is a member of NSA and is part of their Million Dollar Speakers Group. In addition to speaking regularly in corporations, colleges and seminars, Dave is a keynote speaker at Get Motivated events across the nation. He is founder and president of Dave Martin International which champions principle-based coaching by connecting, encouraging, and investing in business leaders, rising entrepreneurs, and anyone desiring a life of more.

## *Dave's Most Popular Topics:*

- Leadership Traits of the Greats
- Seven Decisions that will Determine Your Success
- Mindset Matters - Your Attitude is more Important than Your Assets

*"The common denominator in both championship athletes and successful individuals is a coach. I highly recommend letting Dave Martin be your coach."*

**- Grant Hill, NBA All-Star**

**My Notes On Dave Martin:**

**Our events that might be a good fit for Dave:**

TRAVELS FROM:
Orlando, FL

# MIKE MCKINLEY

## *Hired for the fun...paid for the content*

Mike has the experience and expertise that people in business need to succeed from his history as a teenage entrepreneur which led to leadership positions in manufacturing, retail, radio, television, and ownership of a multimillion dollar publishing house, professional speaking, and consulting business.

Hired for the fun but paid for the content, Mike entertains while he teaches – presenting as the keynote speaker at corporate trainings, in-house programs, and for professional association meetings. An example of his client list includes Great Clips, The Toro Company, Subway, Gillette, and American Family. Hundreds of companies – from construction to healthcare, high technology to the auto industry- have relied on Mike for insight into furthering today's business growth, innovation, and success.

Mike uses real life photos for fun and humor yet ties them into serious points about life and changing business. Mike's performance ingredients (topics) include Change, The Customer Journey, Maximizing Performance, Teamwork, Leadership, Motivation, and Balancing Work & Home. Working with Mike's consulting clients and his vast array of businesses gives him a breadth of real life experience and business expertise on which to draw when he shares his ideas and performs for you.

It's time to think fresh thoughts and seek new perspectives

### Mike's Most Popular Topics:

- Transforming Today's Challenges into Tomorrow's Business
- Together We're Even Better...You Make the Difference
- Leadership for Today and Tomorrow

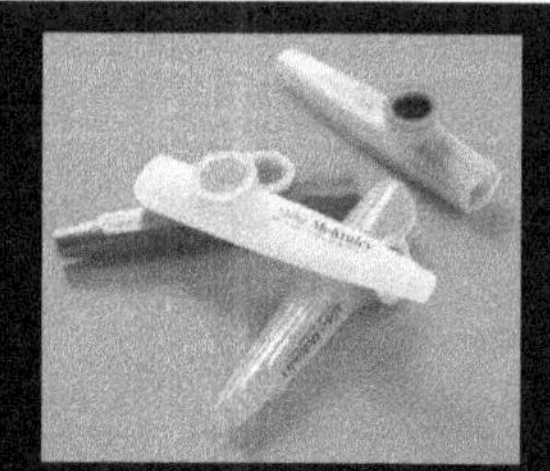

*"Not only were you one of the best speakers we can remember having at Congress ... Your rapid-fire presentation, punctuated with some incredible, funny and thought provoking visuals, laced powerful business and life insights with hilarious stories and photos. Of all our keynote speakers, you scored highest and longest on the laugh meter. Yet amid all the humor, you drove home some very useful lessons our members could take home."*

**- Dan Maddux
Executive Director, American Payroll Association**

**My Notes On Mike McKinley:** _______________________

_______________________________________________________

_______________________________________________________

_______________________________________________________

_______________________________________________________

_______________________________________________________

_______________________________________________________

_______________________________________________________

_______________________________________________________

_______________________________________________________

_______________________________________________________

_______________________________________________________

_______________________________________________________

_______________________________________________________

_______________________________________________________

**Our events that might be a good fit for Mike:** _______________________

_______________________________________________________

_______________________________________________________

_______________________________________________________

_______________________________________________________

TRAVELS FROM:
Minneapolis/Orlando

# Dr. Romie Mushtaq, MD

## *Stress Healer: Medicine Meets Mindfulness*

Dr. Romie Mushtaq, MD is a physician, mindfulness expert, speaker, and media personality who brings together medicine and mindfulness to help individual clients and corporations conquer stress, find happiness, and boost productivity.

She is a traditionally trained neurologist with additional board certification in Integrative Medicine. She completed her medical training at the Medical University of South Carolina, University of Pittsburgh Medical Center, and the University of Michigan.

After suffering from career burnout and undergoing life-saving surgery, she traveled around the world learning mindfulness-based techniques. Dr. Romie combines her unique expertise in neuroscience & mindfulness as a highly sought after speaker to teach stress management and mindful leadership to Fortune 500 companies, universities and associations around the country. She also helps patients achieve brain & mental health holistically at the Center for Natural & Integrative Medicine in Orlando, Florida.

Dr. Romie's expertise has been featured on TED talks, Fox News, NBC, NPR, The Huffington Post, and dozens of other national media outlets. She is currently writing her first book on bringing Western Medicine & Eastern Wisdom together for a "Busy Brain Cure."

*Dr. Romie*

### *Dr. Romie's Most Popular Topics:*

- **Mindset Matters: 5 Mindful Steps to Conquering Stress**
- **Mindful Leadership: Navigating Chaos to Calm**
- **De-Spanx: Breathe Purpose & Passion Back into Your Life**

*"Dr. Romie has a heart-warming and down-to-Earth style. She has spoken at four Fidelity Investment events in 2016 with several requests to bring her back. Her voice and message on stress management, life-work balance, and mindful leadership draws in the entire room of executives. I can't thank her enough for being a part of our meetings, she is a very special person, and her impact is far reaching in our organization."*

**– L. Thomas, Manager, PWI Meetings & Client Events, Fidelity Investments**

**My Notes On Dr. Romie Mushtaq:** _______________________

**Our events that might be a good fit for Dr. Romie:** _______________

**TRAVELS FROM:**
Orlando, FL

# Jim Pancero CSP, CPAE

If you are excited, motivated and ready to improve your sales success, then Jim Pancero has the powerhouse, leading-edge solutions  you need to increase your competitive sales advantage.

A leading go-to sales strategist for more than 30 years, Jim has been influencing, guiding and inspiring sales professionals in more 80 different industries to increase sales and market share. Jim's combination of humor, larger-than-life personality, outstanding research and real-world examples that hit home provide even experienced sales pros who think they've heard it all with strategies and concepts that work!

Your sales team will be charged up and ready to go...and your company and customers will reap the rewards. Time with Jim is time well spent-- watch your productivity and profitability soar!

### Jim's Most Popular Topics:

- "How to Best Connect and Sell the Millennial Buyer"
- "You Can Always Sell More - Are You Good Enough to Get Even Better?"
- "Will You Be Able to Attract The Best Millennials to Your Sales Team?"
- "Are You Ready For Your Next Generation of Sales Reps?"
- "SWAT Team Selling – Leading Your Team to a Competitive Advantage"

*"We see a benefit, we're seeing it already in our team, our team is responding to it. I've had our rookies thank me so much for the training, and I've had our veterans walk out feeling like they've really learned something new that they can help grow their market. So, where ever your team is, I would say this is not introductory training, this is higher level advanced sales training. If that's what you're looking for, then Jim's your man."*

**- Will Green, Sr. V.P. of Sales, Southeastern Paper Group**

**My Notes On Jim Pancero:** ________________________________________

________________________________________________________________

________________________________________________________________

________________________________________________________________

________________________________________________________________

________________________________________________________________

________________________________________________________________

________________________________________________________________

________________________________________________________________

________________________________________________________________

________________________________________________________________

________________________________________________________________

________________________________________________________________

________________________________________________________________

________________________________________________________________

________________________________________________________________

________________________________________________________________

**Our events that might be a good fit for Jim:** ___________________

________________________________________________________________

________________________________________________________________

________________________________________________________________

________________________________________________________________

________________________________________________________________

________________________________________________________________

________________________________________________________________

TRAVELS FROM:
Dallas, TX

# MARY A. REDMOND

## - *The FearLess Negotiator*

Audiences choose Mary to share common sense negotiation tips and processes that work for every organizational level. Her stories are fresh from the negotiation trenches and are chocked full of humor and humility.

Following a 22-year career with Fortune 500 banks and financial institutions, she's traveled the world working with C-level executives, managers and staff sharing her Negotiation and Communications expertise.

"She developed The H.E.A.R.D. Process™, a 5-Step plan to achieve more of what you want at work and in your personal relationships by following a guiding belief. "If You Don't Ask You Don't Get."

The techniques and tips she shares are based on years of careful observation of human behavior in stressful, high pressure, sales situations and complex contract negotiations.

Her passion for accurately interpreting body language helps audiences learn how to read what others are thinking before they open their mouths.

She's negotiated with aggressive attorneys, angry accountants, egotistical executives, overworked hotel front desk clerks and tow truck driving bullies. That's how she earned the reputation as the FearLess Negotiator.

She lives a life filled with hope, where once there was despair as a long-time recovering alcoholic and brain injury survivor.

## *Mary's Most Popular Topics:*

- If You Don't Ask, You Don't Get. The H.E.A.R.D. Negotiation Process
- Body Language I Don't See What You're Saying
- Listen: Be Brilliant
- Men and Women Do It Differently: Negotiate That Is!

*"Mary Redmond's Fearless Negotiation workshops and presentations have hit the mark for our conference attendees for over 10-years.*

*She understands the complex and stressful negotiations that our Law Firm Administrator members deal with every day. She always shares tips they can implement immediately. Her style is humorous and fast-paced. Her content is custom-tailored to our members. Each story is engaging and our members love Mary. "*

**– Peggy L. Siems,**
**Professional Development Program Manager, Association of Legal Administrators**

**My Notes On Mary A. Redmond:** _______________________________

_______________________________________________________________

_______________________________________________________________

_______________________________________________________________

_______________________________________________________________

_______________________________________________________________

_______________________________________________________________

_______________________________________________________________

_______________________________________________________________

_______________________________________________________________

_______________________________________________________________

_______________________________________________________________

_______________________________________________________________

_______________________________________________________________

_______________________________________________________________

_______________________________________________________________

**Our events that might be a good fit for Mary:** _______________

_______________________________________________________________

_______________________________________________________________

_______________________________________________________________

_______________________________________________________________

_______________________________________________________________

_______________________________________________________________

TRAVELS FROM:
Kansas City, MO

# BILLY RIGGS  *- The World's Only DIS-illusionist!*

Billy Riggs has been called "The Dr. Phil of Magic," and "a psychologist masquerading as a comedian and magician." He was voted one of **America's Top Five Most Entertaining Speakers in a 2014 nationwide poll of conference attendees**. This past June he received a standing ovation from 13,000 people for his inspiring message at the prestigious Million Dollar Roundtable in Orlando, Florida. As a highly skilled orator Billy moves audiences to action with his message of hope and inspiration. Add in his talent as a master magician, illusionist, and spellbinding entertainer, and he delivers a presentation that audiences will remember long after the event ends. Billy's presentations change lives, improve attitudes, turbocharge sales, and inspire exceptional service. Through television, radio, books, videos, and live keynote speeches Billy continues to spread his message, and currently more than a million people on five continents have benefitted from his work. In 2010, Billy starred in his own television special, *The Magic of Attitude*.

Awarded the prestigious CSP designation in 2002, Billy's skill as a professional speaker has been perfected over nearly 4 decades. Audiences are stirred by his sincerity and power on the platform. When Billy Riggs appears, things on stage *disappear*, time flies, and no one leaves the room! Using Las Vegas-quality magic and illusions to drive home his points, Billy's presentations have transformed hundreds of otherwise ordinary conferences into events that are truly special. His quick wit and quicker hands spread laughter and raise morale as listeners learn to reshape their destinies by eliminating their "Grand Illusions" and embracing even grander realities.

## Billy's Most Popular Topics:

- How to Become a Born Leader
- The Magic of Attitude!
- Positively Magical Service!

*"In my seventeen years as a rally producer, a speakers' bureau and a fulltime career planner for major heavyweights in the speaking industry, I've never seen so much talent rolled up into one person as I have with Billy Riggs. Billy has the ability to be as inspirational as Zig Ziglar, as analytical as Stephen Covey, and as entertaining as David Copperfield all at the same time."*
**– Juanell Teague,
Business Coach to the Speaking Industry**

**My Notes On Billy Riggs:**

**Our events that might be a good fit for Billy:**

# KENYON SALO

*"Professional, Funny, Engaging, Daring, Strategic, Hard Hitting, Powerful and Always Memorable!"*

Kenyon Salo is one of the top trainers, facilitators and keynote speakers in his field of adventure, leadership, team building, sales, inspiration and motivation. One of only five members on the Denver Broncos Thunderstorm Skydive Team he is seen each week flying into Sports Authority Field at 60+mph, ending with a soft tip-toe landing on the ten yard line. He brings to the stage over 20+ years of successful audience engagement through humor, awe-inspiring moments, prolific storytelling and 'edge-of-the seat' content. His goal is to deliver high caliber, powerful and heart touching content to each person in the room.

**Fast Facts:**
- Master Trainer and Speaker of more than 100k+ people
- Trainer for a National Social Media Campaign for Fortune 500 Company
- Featured on NFL Films, ESPN, NBC, CBS, ABC, FOX, MTV
- NFL Denver Broncos Thunderstorm Skydive Team
- Performed Stand-Up Comedy at Denver Comedy Works
- Travelled to 49/50 US States and 27+ Countries
- Believes in High Quality and Professional Experiences
- Photographer, Adventure Video Creator
- 5500+ Skydives
- 400+ BASE Jumps

### Kenyon's Most Popular Topics:

- "The Bucket List Life" - Create More Experiences, Share More Stories, and Live More Fulfilled!
- The Difference Is In The Experience! Step by Step Micro View Of The Bucket List Life Model.

*"Kenyon Salo was recently both the opening and closing keynote speaker for our leadership conference, Inspiring Legendary Leaders. In addition we asked him to be the emcee for the event. Although this was a new endeavor for him, he said - confidently - "it's in my wheelhouse." As emcee he was conscience of the timing, easy to work with and engaged the audience. As keynote, he motivated and inspired the participants with stories of The Bucket List Life and gave steps on how they could achieve theirs. His positive high energy and enthusiasm were contagious! As an event planner, I can positively say Kenyon will be an asset to your conference in any capacity."*

**– R.L., Lead Event Planner, Inspiring Legendary Leaders**

**My Notes On Kenyon Salo:** ______________________________

__________________________________________________________

__________________________________________________________

__________________________________________________________

__________________________________________________________

__________________________________________________________

__________________________________________________________

__________________________________________________________

__________________________________________________________

__________________________________________________________

__________________________________________________________

__________________________________________________________

__________________________________________________________

__________________________________________________________

__________________________________________________________

**Our events that might be a good fit for Kenyon:** ______________

__________________________________________________________

__________________________________________________________

__________________________________________________________

__________________________________________________________

__________________________________________________________

__________________________________________________________

TRAVELS FROM:
Denver, CO

# LAUREN SCHIEFFER, CSP
## - *The Colonel's Daughter*

As the daughter of a career Air Force officer, Lauren Schieffer grew up being uprooted and relocated every couple of years. This imbued her with a profound independence and ability to adapt to changing circumstances. The lessons she learned from "The Colonel" have helped her make smart decisions and overcome adversity with humility and a sense of humor.

Lauren has navigated just about every aspect of corporate America in her varied career - from trucking to achieving top-tier Sales Director status for a global cosmetics firm to managing a non-profit foundation. In her speaking career, she has presented in seven countries to associations, organizations, federal, state and local governments, as well as Fortune 500 companies - helping them improve the effectiveness of their communication and reduce unnecessary conflict.

Lauren is a Certified Speaking Professional through the NSA and IFFPS. Able to relate to and energize everyone from the custodial staff to C-Level executives, Lauren is a master storyteller, delivering insightful, inspirational and relevant content that empowers people to absorb and act upon what they've heard – and she does so in an entertaining manner with a dry sense of humor that keeps them chuckling while they're learning.

Her enthusiasm is infectious and her passion unmistakable.

### Lauren's Most Popular Topics:
- Leading Out of Drama® - Creating a Culture of Compassionate Accountability
- Finding Significance - Transcending Success to Achieve Significance
- Before it Comes to Blows! - Managing Conflict from Higher Ground

*"I was blown away by Lauren's passion, infectious attitude and professionalism. Lauren was able to electrify the audience, and set the pace for our animated event. We have a wide array of attendees. Lauren was able to engage all of the audience with ease, and because of her expertise, our audience was able to enjoy every aspect of the event. We look forward to having Lauren again!"*

**- Devin Carter, Chairperson – Touch-A-Truck Annual Gala 2016**

**My Notes On Lauren Schieffer:** ______________________________

_________________________________________________________

_________________________________________________________

_________________________________________________________

_________________________________________________________

_________________________________________________________

_________________________________________________________

_________________________________________________________

_________________________________________________________

_________________________________________________________

_________________________________________________________

_________________________________________________________

_________________________________________________________

_________________________________________________________

_________________________________________________________

_________________________________________________________

_________________________________________________________

**Our events that might be a good fit for Lauren:** ______________

_________________________________________________________

_________________________________________________________

_________________________________________________________

_________________________________________________________

_________________________________________________________

TRAVELS FROM:
Kansas City, MO

# Brian Shapiro

## *Unlock Your Communication Power!*

Growing up in a Los Angeles entertainment industry family, it's easy to understand how Brian Shapiro became utterly fascinated with the human communication process.

From an early age, Brian witnessed communication expertly deployed to spin stories and craft tales that deeply impacted people's lives...for better and for worse!

Now a respected communication thought leader, author, performing artist, and University of Pennsylvania affiliated faculty member, Brian has spent over two decades studying and exploring the human communication process.

Brian weaves tried-and-true research with humor and uplifting storytelling to engage audiences so they can expand their own personal communication practices to thoughtfully capture people's attention and generate a feeling of "being valued" in all those they interact with.

### *Brian's Most Popular Topics:*

- **EXCEPTIONALLY HUMAN™: Successful Communication in a Distracted World**
- **OH, THE STORIES WE TELL: Welcome to the Hollywood of Our Mind**
- **EXTRACT, EXTRACT, EXTRACT! There's Value in Those Interactions!**

*"Brian Shapiro is an impactful change agent! Since working with Brian, we've all experienced and expressed greater empathy, authenticity, and intentionality around making our organization an engine for innovation and creativity."*

**– Karin Copeland, Executive Director, Arts + Business Council & Vice President, Membership Engagement, Chamber of Commerce for Greater Philadelphia**

**My Notes On Brian Shapiro:** ___________________________

_______________________________________________________

**Our events that might be a good fit for Brian:** ___________________

TRAVELS FROM:
Philadelphia, PA

# Jeff Slutsky

## *"The Street Fighter"*
## Doing More With Less

*StreetFighter Influence Booster* is a special approach for increasing the results from all forms of your every day communications. Distilled from the proven principles and approaches behind the most effective and persuasive advertising, sales and public relations strategies, Street Fighter Influence Booster allows you to get your points, positions, proposals and ideas heard, understood and implemented. Whether Volunteer or Vendor; Supervisor, Subordinate or Supplier; Consultant, Co-worker, Colleague or Committee, you dramatically increase the value of your own personal "brand" when things get done by incorporating a few simple, yet effective Street Fighter persuasive communication tactics .

Doing more with less is more important than ever before. Budgets are tighter, resources are stretched and yet expectations for results are high. That's why you need a "Street Fighter!" You need Jeff Slutsky.

*Jeff's Most Poplular Topics:*
- **Street Fighter Influence Booster**
- **Marketing Without Money**
- **Selling Made Super Simple**
- **Advertising On A Shoestring**

## "BRAINS OVER BUCKS"
#### *INC. MAGAZINE*

     PH: 913-488-6480     EMAIL: NANCY@REDPROPS.COM

**MY NOTES ON JEFF SLUTSKY:** ___________________________________

**OUR EVENTS THAT MIGHT BE A GOOD FIT FOR JEFF:** _______________

TRAVELS FROM:
Kansas City, MO

# Dan Stalp

## *Transformational Speaker and Influencing Expert"*

Dan's strength as an impactful speaker begins with the "why" behind the "what" - in becoming the best person you can be. Attendees attracted to Dan's messages:

- Want more life significance through their career and other roles they deem important;
- Desire more gratitude in their life knowing this is the key to more joy and satisfaction; and
- Strive to be the best person possible. They have a gap between where they are and where they want to go – yet want to enjoy where they presently are!

Once Dan inspires you to want more - he gives wise, practical advice on how to get more. He loves audience interaction and receives top marks for his ability to "enter-train"!

## *Dan's Most Popular Topics*

- Career Significance
- The Psychology Behind Influencing People
- The Power of Gratitude

*"What a fantastic keynote... great interaction, interesting facts, and thank you for getting us up and moving!"*

**- Jan Burchett, Executive Director**
**National Association of Remodelers**

   PH: **913-488-6480**   EMAIL: NANCY@REDPROPS.COM

**MY NOTES ON DAN STALP:**

**OUR EVENTS THAT MIGHT BE A GOOD FIT FOR DAN:**

TRAVELS FROM:
Kansas City, MO

# Kelsey Tainsh

Kelsey Tainsh has lived her life differently than she planned, hoped for or dreamed of. By the age of 13, she was a world champion wake boarder and featured on the TV show Entertainment Tonight. She acted in movies including "Rumor Has It" and television shows such as "Gilmore Girls," and "Desperate Housewives."

Despite the daunting challenges she faced, Kelsey graduated from The University of Florida (magna cum laude), worked for The Coca-Cola Company and travels the country as a professional speaker. She appeared on The Diane Jones Morning Show, donned the cover of the National Speaker's Association's (NSA) Speaker Magazine and has been featured in Coca-Cola's Journey, BYOU Magazine, and Business Innovators Magazine. Despite major life-changing medical obstacles, Kelsey brings an upbeat, unique perspective on life, kindness, inclusion and the will to succeed.

## Kelsey's Most Popular Topics

- "I'm Not Limping. That's Swagger! How Shifting Your Perspective Can Boost Your Potential.
- "Pockets: What They Hold What They Hide"
- "Surviving and Thriving Following a Major Medical or Life Setback"

*"I think Kelsey embodies the best that each of us could be: determined, hopeful, positive in the face of physical challenges, and truly desirous of making a difference in the world. These are her strengths, both on and off the platform. When people hear her story and see what she has overcome, they feel like saying, 'Well, I'm done complaining.' She is charming and unafraid. Her humor makes us comfortable with her, and her magnetism makes us love her."*

**– Lou Heckler CSP, CPAE**
**– Speaker Magazine**

**My Notes On Kelsey Tanish:** _______________________________

_______________________________________________________________

_______________________________________________________________

_______________________________________________________________

_______________________________________________________________

_______________________________________________________________

_______________________________________________________________

_______________________________________________________________

_______________________________________________________________

_______________________________________________________________

_______________________________________________________________

_______________________________________________________________

_______________________________________________________________

_______________________________________________________________

_______________________________________________________________

_______________________________________________________________

**Our events that might be a good fit for Kelsey:** _______________

_______________________________________________________________

_______________________________________________________________

_______________________________________________________________

_______________________________________________________________

_______________________________________________________________

TRAVELS FROM:
Atlanta, GA

EXCERPTS FROM:

# FROM THE BIG SCREEN TO THE REAL WORLD

BY JEFF SLUTSKY & LARRY WINGET

## CHAPTER 1
### SLUTSKY & WINGET'S
### FAVORITE HOLLYWOOD QUOTES ON LIFE

*"You can do anything with your life that you want to"*
-ARTHUR,  SIR JOHN GIELGUD (HOBSON)

*"What we do in life, echoes in eternity."*
- GLADIATOR, RUSSELL CROW  (MAXIMUS DECIMUS MERIDIUS)

*"As a matter of cosmic history, it has always been easier to destroy, than to create."*
- STAR TREK II: THE WRATH OF KAHN,  CAPT. LEONARD  NEMOY (SPOCK)

*"I saw my whole life flash before my eyes! ...It was boring!"*
- CHICKEN RUN, JANE HORROCKS  (BABS)

*"He chose....poorly."*
- INDIANA JONES AND THE LAST CRUSADE,  (GUARDIAN KNIGHT)

*"Beginnings are scary. Endings are usually sad, but it's what's in the middle that counts. So, when you find yourself at the beginning, just give hope a chance to float up. And it will."*
- HOPE FLOATS,  SANDRA BULLOCK,  (BIRDEE PRUITT)

*"It's life, Captain, but not life as we know it."*
- STAR TREK, THE MOTION PICTURE,  LEONARD NEMOY  (SPOCK)

*"I happen to believe you make your own destiny. You have to do the best with what God gave you."*
*"What's my destiny, Mama?"*
*"You're gonna have to figure that out for yourself. Life is a box of chocolates, Forrest. You never know what you're gonna get."*
- FORREST GUMP,  SALLY FIELDS TO TOM HANKS

*"Look out for Number One, but don't step in Number Two."*
-BACK TO SCHOOL,  RODNEY DANGERFIELD (THORNTAN MELON)

*"Aren't you grateful that our scars have the power to remind us that the past was real?"*
- RED DRAGON,  ANTHONY HOPKINS (HANNIBAL LECTER)

*"Life's a garden . . . dig it"*
- JOE DIRT,  DAVID SPADE (JOE DIRT)

*"Sucking all the marrow out of life doesn't mean choking on the bone."*
- DEAD POETS SOCIETY,  ROBIN WILLIAMS (JOHN KEATING)

*"Maybe there ain't no sin and there ain't no virtue, they's just what people does. Some things folks do is nice and some ain't so nice, and that's all any man's got a right to say."*
THE GRAPES OF WRATH,  HENRY FONDA

*"You're only young once, but you can be immature forever."*
- MAHOGANY,  ANTHONY PERKINS

*"The future is not set."*
- THE TERMINATOR,  MICHAEL BIEHN  (KYLE REESE)

*"Sometimes you got to lose yourself before you can find anything."*
- DELIVERANCE,  BURT REYNOLDS

**"Have a wonderful time, whoever you're with."**
- HARVEY,  JIMMY STEWART

**"Anything you do could have serious repercussions on future events."**
- BACK TO THE FUTURE,  CHRISTOPHER LLOYD

**"Don't let your mouth get your ass in trouble."**
- SHAFT,  RICHARD ROUNDTREE

**"It's like riding a psychotic horse toward a burning stable."**
- THE BIRD CAGE,  ROBIN WILLIAMS (ARMAND)

*"Value this time in your life kids, because this is the time in your life when you still have your choices, and it goes by so quickly. When you're a teenager you think you can do anything, and you do. Your twenties are a blur. Your thirties, you raise your family, you make a little money and you think to yourself, "What happened to my twenties?" Your forties, you grow a little pot belly you grow another chin. The music starts to get too loud and one of your old girlfriends from highschool becomes a grandmother. Your fifties you have a minor surgery. You'll call it a procedure, but it's a surgery. Your sixties you have a major surgery, the music is still loud but it doesn't matter because you can't hear it anyway. Seventies, you and the wife retire to Fort Lauderdale, you start eating dinner at two, lunch around ten, breakfast the night before. And you spend most of your time wandering around malls looking for the ultimate in soft yogurt and muttering "how come the kids don't call?" By your eighties, you've had a major stroke, and you end up babbling to some Jamaican nurse who your wife can't stand but who you call mama. Any questions?"*
- CITY SLICKERS, BILLY CYRSTAL (MITCH ROBBINS)

# NOTES

# NOTES

## Solution to the Puzzle of Finding the Right Speaker

### *(See Page 9 for Puzzle)*

```
+  +  +  O  B  L  M  E  O  +  R  E  D  A
+  +  +  U  R  U  L  P  N  O  E  U  N  R
+  A  T  N  S  E  O  I  R  I  F  B  O  O
+  Z  N  H  E  C  C  I  R  S  F  A  M  N
+  B  T  T  S  H  P  N  G  C  E  N  D  I
+  A  I  I  H  A  O  G  A  +  I  K  E  N
Q  +  P  R  H  O  I  C  +  P  H  S  R  M
+  E  +  S  O  R  N  +  +  +  C  A  +  A
M  C  K  I  N  L  E  Y  +  +  S  L  +  R
H  C  A  B  R  E  T  U  A  L  +  O  +  T
+  +  +  +  +  +  +  M  A  C  K  E  Y  I
K  A  M  P  S  L  U  T  S  K  Y  +  +  N
H  S  N  I  A  T  +  A  L  L  A  H  B  +
+  +  N  H  A  C  +  +  S  T  A  L  P  +
```

**ie: Name (Over, Down, Direction)**

| | | |
|---|---|---|
| ANTHONY - **2, 3, SE** | EUBANKS - **12, 1, S** | REDMOND - **13, 7 N** |
| ARONIN - **14, 1, S** | FINE - **11, 4, NW** | RIGGS - **6, 8, NE** |
| BHALLA - **13, 13, W** | KAMP - **1, 12 E** | SALO - **12, 7, S** |
| BIRO - **2, 5, SE** | LAUTERBACH - **10, 10, W** | SCHIEFFER - **11, 9, N** |
| BUTZ - **5, 1, SW** | MACKEY - **8, 11, E** | SHAPIRO - **4, 8, NE** |
| CAHN - **6, 14, W** | MARTIN - **14, 7, S** | SLUTSKY - **5, 12, E** |
| COHEN - 8, 7, NW | MCKINLEY - **1, 9, E** | STALP - **9, 14, E** |
| CRILL - **10, 5 NW** | MUSHTAQ - **7, 1, SW** | TAINSH - **6, 13, W** |
| EPISCOPO - **2, 8, NE** | PANCERO - **10, 7, NW** | |

      PH: **913-488-6480**    EMAIL: NANCY@REDPROPS.COM